Gateshead's
Grand Houses Revisited

Sandra Brack, Bob Dixon, Margaret Hall and Helen Ward
Gateshead Local History Society

Foreword

As a Trustee and Custodian of one of the grand houses in this book I have always found it fascinating that in Gateshead, if you know where to look, there are so many more houses which are even grander than Bensham Grove (right). They also have interesting stories to tell.

The great industrialists of the past lovingly built their homes away from the chemical-laden air of the riverside, the dirt of the coal mines, and the noise of the

Image courtesy of Bensham Grove Community Centre.

factories. They built big, fine and fashionable houses hidden within large gardens or on tree-lined streets.

Gateshead's Grand Houses Revisited is taking another look at some of these houses and pointing out others that were not included in the previous book. Great credit must go to the authors, Sandra Brack, Bob Dixon, Margaret Hall, and Helen Ward for their hard work and meticulous research.

Shirley Brown
(Trustee of Bensham Grove)

All proceeds from this publication will go toward
Gateshead Local History Society events and research projects.

Copyright © Gateshead Local History Society 2016

First published in 2016 by

Summerhill Books
PO Box 1210, Newcastle upon Tyne NE99 4AH

www.summerhillbooks.co.uk

email: summerhillbooks@yahoo.co.uk

ISBN: 978-1-911385-00-4

Introduction

In September 2012 Gateshead Local History Society launched their first book *Gateshead's Grand Houses*. The book introduced and shared a great number of halls, houses, villas and mansions of Gateshead to show the wealth and prosperity of the town both yesterday and today. The book also looked at the residents and their ingenuity, their involvement in commerce and development in engineering, mining, and industry.

Due to the popularity of the first book members of Gateshead Local History Society have compiled a second book to share more detail on the interesting houses, villas and mansions of Gateshead. The book contains one or two old favourites from the first book along with new and up to date information. Alongside these are a selection of new notable houses and villas which have an interesting story to tell, and shows the craftsmanship and sustainability of beautiful buildings in our town.

Again this is not an exhaustive collection; hidden away from everyday view are still a number of private residences that we have not been able to include.

We hope you enjoy our collection.

Gateshead Local History Society

Gateshead Local History Society was established in 1964 and celebrated its 50th Anniversary in September 2014. Meetings take place between September and April at 7 pm in Gateshead Central Library with a variety of speakers on both local and regional heritage. Members also plan displays, walks and talks during History Month each year and for the past three years have arranged the Perambulation which is a 13 mile walk of the old Gateshead Boundary. The photograph right shows the final stretch of the Perambulation on Saturday, 23 May 2015.

Image courtesy of Peter Bladon.

In 2014 Gateshead Local History Society was approached by Amberley Publishing to compile a book *Gateshead From Old Photographs*. Three members of the society Sandra Brack, Margaret Hall and Anthea Lang researched and compiled a book that covered the changes in Gateshead throughout the 20th century. *Gateshead From Old Photographs* was launched in September 2015 and can be purchased through the society at £14.99.

The Society is also involved with a 1914 project and is researching Gateshead casualties of the Great War. We have supported Low Fell Forum, Gateshead Library, St Mary's Heritage Group and Sunniside Local History Society with Heritage Lottery Bids. We are currently

supporting Gateshead Council with the relocation of the Maccoy Fountain. The Society will also be taking over the responsibility from Gateshead Council for erecting Blue Plaques in the town which are an historic marker to commemorate a famous person or event.

Ashfield House and Lodge

On 3 September 1863 William Wailes sold the land called 'Far Nancy pit field' to John Mawson, a chemist of Gateshead. Unfortunately in December 1867, John Mawson died as he tried to safely dispose of nitroglycerine explosive on Newcastle Town Moor which had been found in a cellar of a public house in Newcastle. The land was later conveyed to his wife Elizabeth Mawson to build one single dwelling and one double villa.

Ashfield House shown right was later built for the family between East Park Road and Durham Road. On 9 March 1899 Elizabeth Mawson conveyed the land to her three daughters, who gained planning approval on 4 March 1903 for a gate lodge for Ashfield located on East Park Road.

Image courtesy of Gateshead Library Archives.

The photograph below shows how the lodge and surrounding area would have looked in the early 20th century, next to the gated entrance of Ashfield House situated on a pleasant country lane. Ashfield Lodge stood empty and open to vandalism for many years, it was then sold by Gateshead Council and has been recently renovated. Ashfield House remains a children's nursery, and is now called Saltwell Childcare and Education. At the time of publication, the land near Ashfield House that was occupied by the former Springs Health Club is currently for sale.

Image courtesy of Gateshead Library Archives.

Belle Vue House

The photograph that was used for Belle Vue House in the first book *Gateshead's Grand Houses* was later found out to be incorrect. The two photographs below have been kindly provided by the current owner of Belle Vue House showing how the house looks today.

Belle Vue House had been divided into three properties; one wing was a semi-detached house and the other wing was divided into two apartments. The current owner bought the semi-detached house in 1996, then bought one of the apartments in 2006 and converted it back to form part of the original building. The owner then bought the remaining apartment in 2013 and plans are currently in hand to also convert this back into the main building, therefore restoring the house back to its original layout.

Image courtesy of owner.

The south west corner of the house shows the original two storey house with plain wide sash windows and a French door. The rest of the house is of a square Jacobean character. On the west front there is a shield with the inscription 'LAUS DEO' (praise (be) to God). The conservatory was built later.

The photograph below from 6 July 1901 shows Captain and Mrs Chapman having a garden party for their Clarke Chapman employees. Clarke Chapman were marine and electrical engineers and boilermakers. Abel Chapman lived at Belle Vue House from 1880 and became the chairman of Clarke Chapman in 1890 after William Clarke unexpectedly died.

Image courtesy of owner.

Private collection.

Bensham Cottage

Bensham Cottage was on Pianet Lane, as shown in the 1857 Ordnance Survey map below, now Derwentwater Road, Bensham, between Bensham Terrace and Bensham Crescent, about where St Aidan's C of E Primary School is today.

Reproduced with Permission. Ordnance Survey.

The house was a stone built two storey property with an unusual curved shaped single storey room to the left of the front entrance. It also had a lovely large bay window and a square porch with stained glass. The steps up to the front door were stone with ornate balustrade on either side leading to the garden which was laid to lawn with trees and shrubs.

The 1841 census shows Mr James Pollock, aged 60, living at Bensham Cottage with his wife Sarah, aged 57, and one servant. According to the Poll Book of 1853, James Pollock was a magistrate and owned houses and shops in High Street, Gateshead. He had also been the treasurer of Gateshead

Image courtesy of Beamish Museum Archives.

Dispensary between 1832 and 1849 and Mayor of Gateshead in 1837. Having lived at Bensham Cottage for a number of years he moved to Whickham Park, Church Chase to live with his daughter and son-in-law.

The probate index of James Pollock Esq on the 20 May 1867:

The will of James Pollock formerly of Bensham Cottage in the Borough of Gateshead but late of Whickham Park in the Parish of Whickham both in the County of Durham Esquire deceased who died 22 March 1867 at Whickham Park. Effects under £100.

The 1851 census listed Joseph Fairless, aged 57, a coal merchant living at Bensham Cottage with wife Isabella, aged 58, and son John, aged 26, an engineer. Also listed was a live-in servant, a gardener and his family. Mr William Henry Holmes a glass manufacturer purchased Bensham Cottage from James Pollock on 19 May 1859 for £1,200.

The 1881 census shows Mr George Davidson a glass manufacturer living at Bensham Cottage, aged 58, with his wife Jane, aged 57, and sons Thomas, aged 20, William A., aged 15, and one servant. George Davidson and Co. was located at Teams Glass Works, Gateshead-on-Tyne. The company was founded in 1867 by Alderman George Davidson, who was a Gateshead butcher and businessman, to make glass chimneys for paraffin lamps which were becoming increasingly popular as a means of lighting. Having bought a greenfield site, George Davidson built the glassworks from scratch and soon the business flourished, making small bottles and wine glasses.

By 1878 production had increased to include such items as biscuit barrels, salt cellars, tumblers, dishes, plates, jugs, mustard pots and comports. Between January and April 1881 production was halted at the glass works due to a serious fire which destroyed warehouses and processing sheds, although the furnaces themselves were not damaged. The company recovered by purchasing moulds and patterns from the Neville Glassworks which had suffered fire damage the year before, and in 1884 acquired more moulds from W.H. Heppell and Co. and from Thomas Grey and Co. of Carr's Hill glassworks.

In 1886 George Davidson introduced the first annual range of domestic tableware, including jugs, dishes, comports, salad bowls, etc, plus water sets of three tumblers and a jug, and won a Gold medal at the Newcastle exhibition for his glassware in 1887. Davidson was always introducing new ideas and designed about 90% of all new products. He died in 1891 at the age of 68. At that time the company was producing between 200 and 250 tons of glassware per month. After his death his son Thomas took over running the company.

Bensham Grove

Bensham Grove is situated on Sidney Grove, off Bensham Road and is a Grade II listed building. The house was purchased by Joshua Watson, a Quaker and cheesemonger who lived over his shop in Newcastle. His son Joseph enlarged Bensham Grove and Robert Spence Watson, his grandson, added Arts and Crafts elements to the rooms resulting in an eclectic mix of Georgian and Victorian features. Robert died in 1911 and upon the death of Elizabeth his wife in 1919 the house became an Educational Settlement before moving on into the care of the Gateshead Education Authority in 1947. During the Second

Image courtesy of Gateshead Library Archives.

World War, a Public Air Raid Shelter which could accommodate 200 people was located within the grounds of Bensham Grove.

In March 2012, Bensham Grove was awarded a Heritage Lottery Fund of around £280,000 towards the restoration of the main building, focussing on the repair and restoration of the historic and architecturally significant Victorian interiors of Bensham Grove.

The scheme was designed to enable the current and future use of the building and its historic character to fully complement each other and move forward together. The retrieval of the historic interiors has provided an outstanding example of Victorian domestic design which can be enjoyed by the whole community.

The photograph left shows the new tiled floor of the conservatory at Bensham Grove which has been designed by members of the groups at the centre.

Image courtesy of Bensham Grove Community Centre.

Bensham Lodge

Bensham Lodge was situated on the corner of what is now Victoria Road and Lobley Hill Road, a used car garage stands on the site today. The lodge can be seen in the 1857 Ordnance Survey map below.

Reproduced with Permission. Ordnance Survey.

An early recording of Bensham Lodge was on 8 February 1839 which was an advert for the sale of household furniture of the late Miss Thomas. Elizabeth Thomas was a spinster, and left an estate worth £7,000 and bonds to the value of £14,000. This was granted to William Spurrell, a residuary legatee substituted in the will as the sole executrix Elizabeth Spurrell had died.

A later resident of Bensham Lodge was Robert Stirling Newall of Newall-Pattinson who married Mary, the youngest daughter of Hugh Lee Pattinson on 14 February 1849 at Boldon. Newall and Pattinson were in partnership. During the 1850s Joseph Edward Hepple lived at Bensham Lodge.

The trade directories for 1870 to 1880 show Mr John Pattinson, an analytical chemist, living at Bensham Lodge whose business address was 75 The Side, Newcastle. The 1871 census records six Pattinson children living at Bensham Lodge with a nurse, cook and housemaid. Of the five girls and one boy, the eldest child was 12 years old and the youngest child, Bertha, was three months old. Mr John Pattinson and his wife must have been away from home the day the census was recorded. Later, Pattinson who was married to a sister of Joseph Wilson Swan, moved to Shipcote House and died in 1912. The 1881 census shows Mr Mark Archer, a coal fitter, ship owner and manufacturer, living at Bensham Lodge with his wife Isabel. By the late 1880s Archer had moved to Farnacres.

The trade directory for 1887/88 lists Miss Jane Joicey living at Bensham Lodge. When she died on 1 February 1896 she left £30,259 17s. Then the trade directories for 1903 to 1908 show Mr Thomas Abbott Rycroft, an accountant with Sir W.G. Armstrong, Whitworth and Company Ltd, at Bensham Lodge. The trade directories from 1909 to 1916 show Mr Frederick Charles Foster, a physician, the 1918 shows Mr E. Barnes a surgeon, then the 1925 Mr Joseph Wilfred Craven a surgeon.

Craven was born 22 November 1888 in Gosforth, Newcastle. He was educated at Bede School in Durham and also Durham University where he graduated MB, BS in 1912. He worked at the Royal Victoria Infirmary, Newcastle and later as a ship surgeon for the P&O Steam Navigation Company. During the First World War Craven served with the 1st Northumberland Field Ambulance, he won the Military Cross, and was appointed a Chevalier of the Legion of Honour and was mentioned in dispatches.

Craven emigrated to New Zealand and in 1939 was appointed to the command of Queen Alexandra Hospital in Singapore. In 1942 he was taken prisoner. During that time his health suffered and he returned to New Zealand in 1945 where he resumed his medical duties, but owing to ill health he resigned in 1949. Craven died on 19 July 1961.

Birchholme

Birchholme is a large stone built house situated at the bottom of The Drive, off Durham Road. Planning permission for the house was approved on 3 May 1899 for Mr John Samuel Leybourne where he later lived with his wife, two daughters and three servants. Leybourne was a coal fitter and general manager of the Priestman Collieries Ltd for sixteen years. The trade directory for 1937 records Mr A.C. Nicholson, a coal exporter, living at Birchholme. In later years, the house was owned by Gateshead Council and was used by the Social Services Department.

Gateshead Council sold Birchholme in the early 2000s.

Birchholme was purchased in 2013 by the current owners. Having stood empty for over ten years it was dilapidated and in serious need of repair. Unfortunately, time had taken its toll and the entire roof, windows, stairs and all internal structures were lost. The house needed to be taken back to the original stonework.

Great care has been taken to restore the house in keeping with the original design, whilst at the same time

Image courtesy of owner.

the house has been brought up to modern standards, with low energy requirements. The inappropriate extensions have been removed and replaced with more respectful structures and the gardens are now undergoing extensive renovation.

Briermede

Briermede was near the present Briermede Avenue off Earls Drive. On 1 December 1875 planning permission was approved for Joseph Grey, a timber merchant, who lived at Briermede for more than forty years. Grey retired at the age of 80; he was a Freeman of Newcastle and one of the original trustees of Jesmond Parish Church. Grey died, aged 89, on 3 September 1918. There is a commemorative window in St Helen's Church, Low Fell. His father erected several of the buildings in Grey Street, Newcastle as well as some of the city's churches.

The photograph left shows the impressive stone gateway on Earls Drive that led to the house.

Image courtesy of Bob Dixon.

Carr Hill House

Carr Hill House was situated on the Causeway, Carr Hill and was built sometime after 1766. It was a substantial three storeyed property with gardens laid out to lawn and trees backing onto Pottery Lane. It would appear the house was actually built to accommodate lunatics as the advertisement which appeared in a local newspaper shows:

LUNATICKS

Carr's Hill House on Gateshead Fell
To The Public

We beg leave to inform the Public that we have opened the above HOUSE pleasantly situated about a mile distant from NEWCASTLE, which we have fitted up in elegant manner, with every Accommodation for the reception of LUNATICKS in genteel or opulent circumstances: in this house Persons entrusted to our care shall be treated with the utmost Attention and Humanity. The terms are reasonable.

R. Lambert, W. Keenleyside, H. Gibson, R. Stoddard (surgeons to the Infirmary) Newcastle, 1767.

By the turn of the 19th century the house was a residential property and farm.

Image courtesy of Mrs J.D. Goddard.

Dene House

Dene House is situated on Chowdene Bank and is a semi-detached property with South Dene. The house was built just down from the Old Quarry in the mid to late 19th century.

Before living at Dene House, the 1870/71 trade directory shows Thomas Hedley living at 31 High Street, and the 1873/74 trade directories show Thomas described as a draper living at 27 Union Lane.

By the 1879 trade directory both Thomas and Henry Hedley are recorded as living at South Dene, it is not clear whether the two brothers were living in the same house or if Dene House and South Dene were at one time one property or whether the name of the house was incorrectly recorded for Thomas. Then the 1883/84 trade directory only lists Thomas living at Dene House, (Henry is recorded as living at South Dene) and the 1911 census shows Thomas is still resident at Dene House at the age of 74.

Thomas was born in 1837 and his brother Henry was born in 1841. The brothers were drapers and owned the large store on Gateshead High Street, which can be seen on the right of the photograph below.

By 1918 Thomas Hedley had died as the trade directory only shows Mrs Hedley living at Dene House. On 1 June 1918 Thomas Hedley, aged 41, son of Eliza and the late Thomas Hedley was killed in action at Aveluy Wood. Corporal Hedley is buried at Martinsart British Cemetery, the Somme.

Image used courtesy of owner.

Image courtesy of Gateshead Library Archives.

Eighton Lodge

Eighton Lodge is located at the southern end of Durham Road, Low Fell just before the roundabout leading onto the A1. One of the first owners is listed in the 1851 census as William Barkus, aged 45, a mining engineer born in Northumberland, with his wife Isabella from Bedlington, aged 33, their three children, daughter Mary Ann, aged 6, son Mark, aged 4, and daughter Isabella, aged 2, and two servants.

The 1861 census shows Mark Fryar living at Eighton Lodge, aged 45, with his wife Dorothy, aged 28, three daughters Dorothy, aged 5, a scholar at home, Sarah, aged 3, and Isabella, aged 1 year, also his sister-in-law Isabella Taylor, aged 30, and three servants. Fryar was chief viewer at Teams Colliery and was a partner in the Plashetts Coal Company and one of the principal salt manufacturers on the banks of the Tyne. Mark Fryar died in September 1868, aged 52.

The 1871 and 1881 censuses show Barnabas Fenwick living at Eighton Lodge. Barnabas Fenwick a mining engineer was born in 1843 in Ryton. He had served his apprenticeship under Mr Thomas Emmerson Forster and was manager of the Broomhill collieries at Amble and the Team and Allerdene collieries, retiring in 1883. He died in April 1921 aged 78 at the residence of his only brother John Henry Fenwick, 66 Manor House Road, Newcastle.

A later resident of Eighton Lodge was William Hedley who died on 30 April 1909, aged 51. A memorial to him is located in Lamesley. Hedley was born on 17 March 1858.

Image used courtesy of owner.

The 1911 census shows Ernest H. Kirkup living at Eighton Lodge, aged 23, with two servants. He is described as single and a coal mining engineer.

Paintings courtesy of Hugh Mackay.

The two paintings above show the north and south views of Eighton Lodge. The building was used as a single mothers' refuge during the 1970s and 80s before becoming a care home. Eighton Lodge is now a residential care home set in 1.5 acre gardens with views of the Angel of the North.

Fellside House

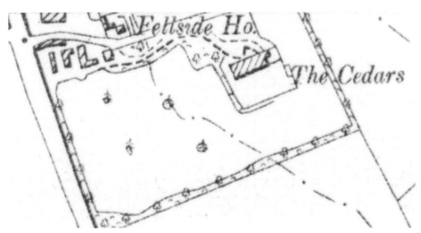

Reproduced with Permission. Ordnance Survey.

Fellside House or Villa was located opposite the Cedars on Blackrow Lane now Ivy Lane, Low Fell, as can be seen on the 1895 Ordnance Survey map left.

The 1873 trade directory shows Mr Carl Layle, a timber merchant, living at Fellside House with his wife Emma. Carl Frederik Leijel (also spelled Layle or Leyel) was born on 1 October 1836 in Nytorp, Sweden. He became the Director for the Swedish

Department of the Newcastle firm of Borries, Craig and Company, who were merchants and shipbrokers, mainly dealing in timber. He married Emma Swan, the daughter of John Swan and Isabella Cameron, on 14 September 1872.

Carl and Emma had two children, a daughter Ethel, born 13 September 1874, and a son Carl Frederik who was born 30 December 1875; both children were born at Fellside Villa. The trade directories for 1873 to 1877 also show Emma's father, John Swan described as a gentleman, living at Fellside Villa. Carl Leyel died 6 February 1876, aged 39, leaving under £1,500, and Emma Leyel continued to live at Fellside to the late 1890s.

Carl and Emma's daughter, Ethel, married Cyril Hitchcock in September 1900 in Hampstead. Their son, Carl Frederik Leyel, married Hilda Winifred Ivy Wauton on 9 September 1900 in St Martin in the Fields, Strand, London, and had two sons Carl Frederik Salvin Leyel, born 6 February 1901, and Christopher Wauton Leyel, born 10 June 1906 in London. After Carl began a relationship in 1921, Hilda petitioned for a divorce.

In 1922 Hilda was prosecuted for running the Golden Ballot. Despite the fact that all profits from the ballots went to helping disabled ex-servicemen, Hilda Leyel found herself facing prosecution under the laws of the Betting and Lottery Acts for running an illegal lottery. The case against her was overthrown, a result that ensured that ballots held solely to raise funds for charitable causes would, from this point forward, be deemed legal across the whole of the United Kingdom.

The actress, political activist, herbalist and charity campaigner Hilda Leyel presented Westfield Memorial village in Lancaster with £20,000 from her second 'Golden Ballot' – the forerunner to the charitable lotteries we know today. A total of 21 cottages were erected of which four conjoined properties were given the name Leyel Terrace.

In the later stages of her life, Hilda's name would become synonymous with herbalism as the founder of the Society of Herbalists. Her only formal honour, a Palmes Academiques, came courtesy of the French Government in 1924.

The 1891 census shows a second family living at Fellside, the family of Dietrich M.L. Wiencke, aged 48, a merchant importer/exporter born in Hanover, Germany. Wiencke became a British subject in 1868.

Field House

Field House is situated on the corner of Windy Nook Road and Queen Elizabeth Avenue, Sheriff Hill. The house is an early to mid-19th century two storey villa constructed of rubble stone, and commands a good sized plot. Field House has been a Grade II listed building since 13 January 1983.

The 1911 census shows Mr Thomas Errington, aged 38, born in Burnopfield, with his wife Elizabeth Rose, aged 39, sons Bertie, aged 19, Thomas, aged 17, daughter Mary Eleanor, aged 16, sons George, aged 12, John Henry, aged 8, William, aged 5 and Elizabeth Rose's aunt Mary Jones, aged 77, all living at Field House.

The later trade directory of 1921 shows a Mrs Daglish living at Field House.

Painting courtesy of owner.

Ford House

Ford House is situated just off Sunderland Road and is now St Wilfred's Presbytery. The house is a 19th century two storey building originally built for George Thornton France, by the architects Austin & Johnson in 1868. Ford House was one of the few substantial stone properties in the area. The 1871 census shows George Thornton France, aged 34, living there with his wife Martha, aged 32, who was born in Newcastle. At the time they had three daughters, Emma, Ethel and Alice and one son, George H., aged 3, and the family had two servants.

The 1881 census shows that the family are still living there. George is listed as a manager of chemical works at Friars Goose. George and Martha now have two more sons and two more daughters and also a 14 year old niece, two servants and a nurse living with them.

The 1891 census lists George and his second wife, Harriet Lucy Stogdon of The Old Vicarage, Heworth-on-Tyne, and their son Walter Frederic who was born at Ford House on 15 February 1887. Walter was educated at Newcastle Grammar School and attended Gonville and Caius College on 1 October 1905, where he gained a BA in 1908. He became the Archbishop of Canterbury's Missionary Exhibitioner in 1905, and was a Missionary in Japan and Ordained Deacon (Japan) in 1910.

George and Harriett also had a daughter Eleanor, born 30 November 1894. Eleanor trained to be a nurse and went to India in October 1924. It would appear she served in the military medical service during the Second World War in Burma and was awarded campaign medals including the Burma Star, and the Kaisar-i-Hind, a decoration granted by the Indian Government for public service. She was also awarded Queen Elizabeth II's Coronation Medal in 1953 for her public service at the Afghan Mission Hospital in Peshawar, North West Province, India (which later became Pakistan). Eleanor returned to England in 1954.

Image used courtesy of owner.

The Sunderland Daily Echo of Monday, 11 August 1902 recorded the death of Mr George Thornton France JP of Ford House, Gateshead, which occurred somewhat suddenly on Sunday, 10 August at Newbiggin-by-the-Sea. France at one time had been the chairman of the Gateshead School Board.

The trade directory for 1911 shows Mr J.W. Kay living at Ford House. The house later became a Presbytery as the 1915 to 1918 trade directories show the Rev. W.J. Goundry living in the house, the 1925 shows Rev. D. McManemy and Rev. W.T. O'Donnell, then the 1929 to 1939 trade directories show the Rev. W.A. Dickinson and the Rev. H. Henry living at Ford House.

The photograph left shows the last of the many stained glass windows that the house once had.

Image used courtesy of owner.

Garden Villa

Garden Villa was situated near the bottom of Split Crow Road, west of Fife Street. The Ordnance Survey map below shows the location in 1857.

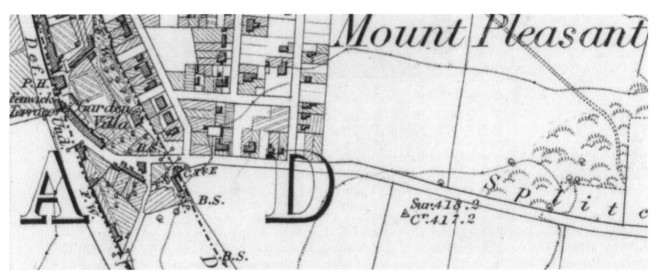

Reproduced with Permission. Ordnance Survey.

A resident of Garden Villa in 1850 was Mr Matthew Maughan, a leather cutter with premises at 182 High Street, Gateshead. By 1853 he had changed occupation to a lamp black manufacturer at Heworth Shore. The 1861 census lists Matthew Maughan of Garden Villa, Fenwick Terrace (part of Split Crow Road), aged 51, with his wife Mary, aged 51, their daughter Mary Ann, aged 21, daughter Margaret, aged 19, son John G., aged 15, daughter Isabella, aged 14, and sons Matthew, aged 11 and James, aged 10.

The 1861 census also lists Samuel Holmes, aged 33, a weighing machine maker from Liverpool living at Garden Villa with his wife Esther, aged 28 (eldest daughter of Matthew and Mary Maughan), who married in February 1851, and their daughters Mary, aged 9, Ann, aged 7, and Elizabeth, aged 4, and one domestic servant.

Matthew died on 21 September 1869 at Garden Villa leaving the sum of £600. The executors to his will were his two sons John George Maughan and Matthew Humble Maughan, both lamp black manufacturers. The trade directory for 1874 shows John George and Matthew Humble Maughan as paint and varnish manufacturers still living at Garden Villa. Matthew Humble Maughan married Sarah Batey on 7 August 1877. After Matthew died on 8 August 1901, leaving £5,599 7s 9d, Sarah continued to live at Garden Villa.

Glenside (Fellside)

Glenside, later renamed Fellside, is a large semi-detached property built of stone with a lovely square bay window on the ground floor. Through an attractive garden, solid stone steps lead up to the front entrance. The house was designed by architect William Lister Newcombe around 1874; he also designed Wellwood, Hillcroft North and South, Mayfield Villa, Westover, Harewood and Hillside at the same time, and Underfell the year after. These houses were ideally situated for the newly opened Low Fell railway station on the Team Valley line which opened in 1868.

On 1 May 1874, Thomas John Jamieson Bell and George Ellison (builders) secured the leasehold from the Right Honourable Henry Thomas Liddell, Lord of Ravensworth, for 99 years on two pieces of land on what is now Saltwell Road South, opposite Belle Vue Bank, with the power to erect eight semi-detached villas. The yearly rent of £72 was to be paid in four equal quarterly payments on 1 August, 1 November, 1 February and 1 May in every year without any deduction.

Within 18 calendar months, from 1 May 1874, at their own cost they had to erect substantial stone walls or wooden or iron fences, four feet in height on all sides of the said pieces of ground which at all times throughout the lease was to be kept in good repair. The lease required the builder to erect four semi-detached villas within 18 months and a further four semi-detached villas within two and half years from 1 May 1874 and expend in the erection of each semi-detached house the sum of £900 at the least. The villas were also required to be insured for at least £600 each. Further, the agreement stipulated:

Image courtesy of owner.

At all times during the lease, maintain and keep so much of the said pieces of ground as should not for the time being be built upon, as ornamental land or as vegetable, flower or fruit gardens and plant the same with suitable trees and shrubs and cultivate the same accordingly.

On 11 July 1874 the builders T.J.J. Bell and G. Ellison agreed the sale and mortgage the leased land to Robert Scott Hopper, a gentleman and solicitor of Newcastle. Hopper also bought the first two properties during their construction, later known as Wellwood and Glenside, for the sum of £3,000.

The area that Glenside covered was 2,465 square yards, being 148' 8" along the east side which later became Saltwell Road South by 196' 6" from east to west; the plot then curves round what is now Station Road. Also included was a small plot of land between Station Road and Breckenbeds Road.

The 1893/94 Whellan directory shows Mr John Archibald Dixon, a solicitor, at Glenside where he lived with his wife Isabella Charlton Bell until about 1904 before moving to Tynemouth. Isabella Charlton Bell was born in 1866, the younger sister of Allison Sutherland Bell who lived next door at Wellwood. The directory for 1906 then lists Mr Hugh Angus, a hide merchant, living at Glenside until about 1910 when he moved to Eslington Villa on Station Road.

In 1911 Mr John Thomas Dunn, an analytical and consulting chemist, aged 52, and his wife Frances, aged 53, were living at Glenside, which was then called Fellside. Dunn was born in 1859 and married Frances Ann Elizabeth Thomas in 1884; they had one daughter Laura, born 1885. In 1901 he became a partner in the firm J. & H.S. Pattinson, Analytical and Consulting Chemists in Newcastle, and by the time of his death in 1939 he was the senior partner. Dunn moved to Thornhill Gardens, Sunderland in 1923.

Mr G. Laverick, a gentleman, moved into Fellside (Glenside) and, by 1931, Mr J.W. Porter, Gateshead's Town Clerk, lived there.

Harewood House

Harewood House was built on one of the two pieces of land leased from Lord Ravensworth by Robert Scott Hopper who purchased the lease from builders, Thomas John Jamieson Bell and George Ellison in 1874.

The land covered an area of 2,275⁶/₉ square yards, being 101' 2" along the east side which later became Saltwell Road South, by 207' 6" from east to west and 102' 4" along the west side which later became Breckenbeds Road. Harewood was built as a semi-detached property with Hillside to the design of architect William Lister Newcombe, to take in the views of the Ravensworth Estate, and incorporated a monumental stone bay, solid stone steps through attractive terraced gardens and attractive hood moulding as can be seen in the photograph right.

John Marriner Redmayne, a gentleman and alkali manufacturer, bought Harewood in 1900, having moved from South Dene Tower. John Marriner Redmayne had married Jane Anne Studdert,

Image courtesy of owner.

daughter of Admiral John Fitzgerald Studdert and Anne Welsh, on 14 February 1857. John Marriner Redmayne was the great-great-grandfather of the actor Edward John David Redmayne who played Stephen Hawking in 'The Theory of Everything'. John Marriner Redmayne died at Harewood on 12 May 1903 and his will appointed Francis John Tennant, his son-in-law, and John Ernest Laidlay as executors. His obituary was recorded in the Yorkshire Post and Leeds Intelligencer on 13 May 1903:

The death occurred yesterday at his residence Harewood, Low Fell, Gateshead, of Mr John Marriner Redmayne, who was a notable figure in North country commercial circles. He was the third son of the late Mr Giles Redmayne, of Brathay Hall, Lancashire and was 73 years of age. After being educated at Tonbridge School and Paris, he went to the North of England as a partner in the firm of H.L. Pattinson and Co., owners of the Felling Chemical Works and had a good deal to do with the chemical trade on the Tyne. Subsequently he entered the timber trade, becoming a principle in the firm of Redmayne and Co. He was one of the founders of the Newcastle Exchange.

Living in Gateshead he interested himself in the municipal affairs, and was elected Mayor in 1870. He was a Justice of the Peace for Durham County and the oldest magistrate on the Tynemouth Bench. Before going to the North he had taken part in London philanthropic work, and on Tyneside he proved equally energetic. He assisted to start the Wellesley training ship and the Northern Counties Orphanage at Newcastle. The institutions for the blind and the deaf and dumb also received his support. The Durham College of Science at Newcastle numbered him among its founders and governors.

A liberal churchman, he joined with the late Mr Hugh Lee Pattinson and Mr R.R. Redmayne in building and endorsing Christ Church, Felling, while he also gave generously to other church extension movements. In politics he supported the late Mr Joseph Cowen. He leaves a widow, five sons and three daughters. The funeral will take place on Friday at Brathay.

In 1904 Tennant and Laidlay made a mortgage agreement with Edith Pratt and Adolphus Havergal Dickinson, who in 1915 transferred the remaining mortgage debt to Charles William Ware of Ripon, a gentleman. In June 1917 Charles William Ware died at Ripon and his will appointed Sarah Maria Ann Ware of Middleham House, Ripon, spinster and Public Trustee as executors. After her death on 22 May 1935, Aldolphus Havergal Dickinson and Public Trustee were appointed executors of the will.

In 1920 Harewood was sold as leasehold subject to the remainder of the original lease of 99 years to Frederick William Bowman, a company's manager and Emily Bowman a spinster. In 1931 they sold Harewood to Ralph Shaw, a manager of 'The Garth' Cleasby Gardens, Low Fell, at which time he also purchased the land freehold from H.A. Sisson and F.G.H. Bedford. In July 1945 Ralph Shaw, then of 53 Bertrand Road, Bolton, sold Harewood to Clifford Shaw, a consulting chemist of 7 Braeside Avenue, Sevenoaks, Kent, who sold the house in 1946 to Thomas Henry Humble. Humble was a partner in the firm of Rickman and Thomas, manufacturers of bakery sundries and flavouring essences, at Queensway, North Eastern Trading Estate, Teams. The company was dissolved on the 15 January 1940.

Harewood was sold to J.G. Spotswood Limited (builders & contractors) of 2 Heaton Road, Newcastle, in January 1949. The approval for the conversion of Harewood into three flats had been granted on 2 December 1948.

In 1954 Harewood was sold to Mrs Lilian Mary Weatherly the wife of Frederick Charles Weatherly of 11A Beaconsfield Road, Low Fell. Harewood was made into four flats at some point between 1948 and being sold in 1963. In 1960 the garden land to the north side of Harewood was sold to Mr G.E. Robson, a builder, for the construction of a new house, 'Anncroft'. Harewood was then sold to Mr G.E. Robson in 1963 and remained as four flats until around 1990, after which it was converted back to a single dwelling by the owners. Harewood is also on Gateshead Council's Local List of notable buildings (ref X20/LL/211).

Heathfield House

Heathfield is situated on Durham Road and was a two storey villa with thirteen rooms built for Joseph Willis Swinburne who gained planning approval on 4 August 1856. In May 2012 the house, then comprising of five flats, was empty and the gateway railed off. Since then Heathfield House has been converted into four luxury apartments with attractive gardens.

Image courtesy of Gateshead Library Archives.

The house has a communal hallway with a tiled floor and a turning staircase with original style bannister. The beautiful gateway situated on Durham Road has been restored providing access via electric gates, and the lions can both be seen in their splendid position on either side.

Prior to renovation an archaeological investigation was undertaken within the grounds of the house where a number of out-buildings were located, which were later demolished in order to build Heathfield Lodge. The outbuildings located to the north of the house included a substation which may have served the mansion or been an energy company substation on private property. There was also a laundry, a coal store, a potting room, a single storey cart shed, stables and carriage house.

The largest room in the service building range was the laundry, so-called for the set-pot against the wall with an iron lintel and a grate next to a large and impressive fireplace range, which had a central fire grate and a small set pot in a round headed alcove to the left and a work surface with a vertical cast iron plate backing to the right (photograph below left).

Images courtesy of AAG Archaeology.

The stables main building (above right) was divided into three bays. The first, easternmost bay contained a blocked room with garage doors opening onto the property to the north. The second, middle bay contained the double door of the main stables with a single window and three stable partitions moulded in concrete on the floor and corresponding with these on the south facing wall were three feed chutes and three tying rings. The hatches for the feed chutes were still above in the hayloft floor. The third bay contained only the double door of another stable or carriage house. The log book of a Civil Defence and National Fire Service motor vehicle, registration PCN 831, was found in the main stable and the entries suggest some kind of Civil Defence Vehicle was stationed there around 1961. This is entirely possible as the building was owned by Gateshead Corporation at the time. Ashfield, next door to Heathfield, was a Civil Defence post and, nearby, South Dene Tower was the ARP centre during the Second World War. The vehicle may have been housed in the recently demolished garage built on the site of the Durham Road lodge, which stood on the south side of the tradesmen's entrance gates. The lodge was still standing and occupied in 1956 but may have been demolished and the garage built between that date and 1961. The site would not have been ideal for garaging a public service vehicle due to the narrow space and gradient.

There was also a blocked up room, possibly an old stable converted to a tack room or groom's quarters which housed an old two-cylinder freestanding gas radiator (right) or parlour stove. The whole appliance was about 1 metre tall and consisted of 850 mm tall cylinders on a 160 mm tall base. The cylinders had a decorative pattern on

Image courtesy of AAG Archaeology.

them. The parlour stove probably dates to the turn-of-the-century or first two decades of the 20th century. There was also a gas light fitting on the wall with the ceramic nozzle still intact (right).

The survival of the stable features was illustrative of a well-designed stable block. The length and complexity of the service building range and the way it was hidden away in the fall of the slope to the side of the house is also significant and testifies to the size of

Image courtesy of AAG Archaeology.

the Heathfield household and garden in its prime. The waste water cistern's survival also underscored the size of the gardens and the necessity and ingenuity of well-placed engineering required in such a household economy.

Hill House

Located on Belle Vue Bank, adjacent to Belle Vue House gates, Hill House (c. 1820) is a three storey end terrace Georgian property adjoining Belle Vue Terrace. It features double bay elevations and dormer windows and has a pleasant garden to the front of the property.

Mr Thomas Bell, surveyor and Town and County stationer, once owned the whole plot of land between Belle Vue Bank, opposite what is now St Helens Crescent, and Alumwell Lane. The remaining land was divided into plots which he rented out. An early payment of 5 shillings per year was the cost for a plot or piece of ground.

The earliest known records state release of deeds on 4 April 1820 from Mr Thomas Bell to Mr Robert Maving and Frances Seymour at Home Villa, 2 Belle Vue Terrace (renamed 'Bell House' in 1974 by the current owners); and one day later on 5 April 1820 from Mr Thomas Bell to Mr Robert Maving at Hill House, 1 Belle Vue Terrace.

One record of 1827 states 'release of a cottage and premises on Gateshead Low Fell from Mr Robert Maving to Mr Thomas Mable'. At that time Robert Maving was leasing the land from Thomas Bell.

A record on 23 May 1853 declared Mr John Todd living at Hill House to be 'a bankrupt' due to owing money to Mr William Charlton of

Image courtesy of owner.

the White Hart Inn, Newcastle. The property went to the highest bidder, being Mr Thomas Bell, who bid £700 for the property.

Records on 12 November 1853 show the lease from Mr Thomas George Bell Esq to Benjamin Kurt Esq. Then, on 31 July 1857, Benjamin Kurt to Emerson Muschamp Bainbridge, draper and founder of the famous 'Bainbridge' Store. £540 is recorded for the conveyance of ground and messuage or dwelling house and premises situate at Low Fell.

The photograph below is of the Deeds, dated 22 July 1864, of Emerson Muschamp Bainbridge conveying the ground and messuage and or premises situate at Low Fell, Gateshead to John Sanjen Baker.

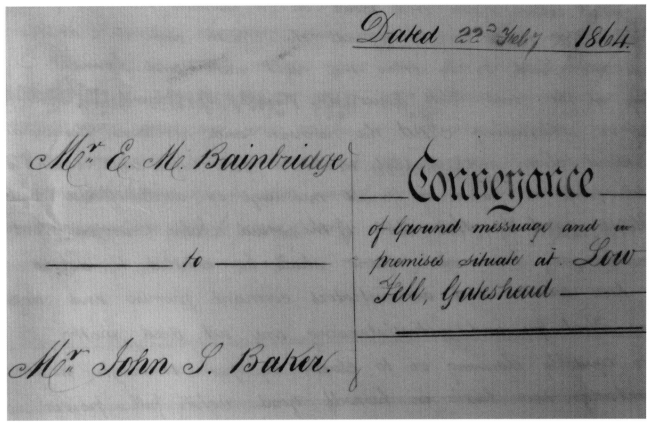

Image used courtesy of owner.

The 1881 census shows John Sanzen Baker living at 1 Belle Vue Terrace, Hill House, Low Fell. John Sanzen Baker was a pork butcher born in 1818 in Baden-Wurttemberg, Germany. He arrived in England on 15 April 1840 and changed his name from Johannes Sazenbacher to John Sanzen Baker. He married Elizabeth Teal on 25 December 1844 and they had nine children. In 1891 he was still living at Hill House, described as a gentleman, with wife Elizabeth and one son, Alfred Henry Sanzen Baker, aged 27, a chemist and druggist, and one servant. John wrote his will at Hill House on 18 December 1889 and died just two months later on 1 February 1890. Probate was granted to John Robert Sanzen Baker, pork butcher, George William Sanzen Baker, pawnbroker and Alfred Henry Sanzen Baker, chemist. John Sanzen Baker left the large sum of £48,468 16s 11d.

By 1907/08 Mr Spraggon, Freeman of the City of Newcastle and much respected gentleman, and his wife Mrs M.A. Spraggon lived at Hill House. The 1918 to 1921 trade directories show Mr William James Greener, recorded as notary public living at Hill House, then by 1929 Mr F.G. Askew lived there.

By 1948 the owners were Major Andrew J. Lamb and his wife Mrs Elsie Lamb, as on 14 July 1948 Articles of Agreement were made between:

Major Andrew J. Lamb of 128 Moorside North, Fenham, Newcastle (the employer) and Messrs John T. Bell & Sons Ltd of 17 Brunswick Place, Newcastle (the contractor) to convert Hill House into two houses at a cost of just £480.

After the house was split into two self-contained houses they were known as Hill House and 1 Belle Vue Terrace. 1 Belle Vue Terrace is directly attached to the rear of Hill House. Whilst Mr and Mrs Lamb lived at Hill House until 1983, they continued to rent out 1 Belle Vue Terrace until 1980, when it was sold and became a private dwelling.

Hillcroft North and Hillcroft South

Hillcroft North and Hillcroft South were built on land leased from Lord Ravensworth by Robert Scott Hopper who purchased the lease from builders, Thomas John Jamieson Bell and George Ellison, on 11 July 1874. The plot covered an area of 6,110$\frac{1}{3}$ square yards being 167' along the east side, which later became Saltwell Road South, by 235' from east to west and 255' along the west side, which later became Breckenbeds Road.

Robert Scott Hopper completed the six semi-detached villas, to the design of William Lister Newcombe. He then sold two of the villas and the grounds attached on 1 November 1878 to Isabella Moorhouse and Samuel Southern, an iron merchant, and they were duly assigned to an annual ground rent of £54. These two properties became Hillcroft North and Hillcroft South and were built in the same style as Wellwood and Glenside.

The 1881 census lists Elizabeth Southern, a widow aged 54, living at Hillcroft with her widowed daughter, sister-in-law, two nieces, a visitor and two servants. The census also lists five 'Hillcrofts' as being uninhabited which may suggest that Hillcroft North and South may have been split into apartments at that time. Hillcroft North and South also had their own Lodge which provided laundry facilities and staff accommodation.

On 5 November 1907 Lord Ravensworth sold the ownership of the land to James Arnott Sisson. Sisson, formerly of Hillcroft, died in 1927 leaving Maria Sisson as sole executrix. After her death in 1929, her will was executed by her son Henry Arnott Sisson, a chartered accountant and son-in-law Frederick Gordon Hay Bedford, an engineer. Bedford was co-inventor in a number of patents for Parsons engineering firm.

Over the years part of the land Hillcroft North and South were built on was sold off. Four semi-detached houses were later built leading down Station Road and a row of houses built along what is now Breckenbeds Road.

The trade directories for 1911 to 1921 show Mr Charles H.L. Bell, a merchant, living at Hillcroft South, and Mr James McDonald Manson, a secretary, living at Hillcroft North. The trade directories for 1929 to 1935 show Mr C.M. Henzell, an oil merchant, living at Hillcroft North.

Hillcroft North and Hillcroft South are shown as A on the 1895 Ordnance Survey map right. They are now split into apartments.

A – Hillcroft North and Hillcroft South.
B – Hillside. C – Mayfield Villa.
Reproduced with Permission. Ordnance Survey.

Hillside

Hillside was also built on land leased from Lord Ravensworth by Robert Scott Hopper who purchased the lease from builders Thomas John Jamieson Bell and George Ellison in 1874. The land covered an area of 2,092 square yards being 98' 8" along the east side, which later became Saltwell Road South, by 207' 6" from east to west and 91' along the west side, which later became Breckenbeds Road.

Hillside house (shown as B on the 1895 Ordnance Survey map above) was built as a semi-detached property next to Harewood. The house was part of the eight properties designed by architect William Lister Newcombe in 1874 and were situated facing over towards the Ravensworth Estate in order to take in the views. Newcombe was born on 7 May 1848, and was educated at Dr Bruce's Academy in Percy Street, Newcastle. In 1885 Newcombe, along with William Henry Knowles of Newcastle and Joseph Hall Morton of South Shields, won the competition that was held to produce plans for a new workhouse at High Teams, Gateshead. Newcombe became one of Newcastle's leading architects and his work includes the Royal Victoria Infirmary along with H.P. Adams.

The first tenant of the house named Hillside was Mark Henderson Redhead. Hillside was destroyed by fire sometime during the 1960s and the land was subsequently used to build Brecken Court.

Lindum House

Lindum House was built for Thomas Wright, an Assistant Stores Superintendent for North Eastern Railway, who had gained planning approval on 4 September 1889. In the centre of the roof there were two small chimney stacks which were connected by ornamental metal-work, and so the house was therefore known as the 'House with a Handle'. The drawing right shows this description clearly with the front elevation laid out to lawn, and a footpath leading to the gates on Durham Road. The ornamental metal-work is not there today.

On 8 May 2014 having been a club for around 100 years, the Lindum Club closed. It reopened on Monday, 26 May 2014 as Café @ The Club, but later the purchaser of Lindum House required vacant possession so on Friday, 19 December 2014 the Café closed.

Drawing courtesy of Doreen McNally.

Mayfield Villa

Mayfield Villa was also built on land leased from Lord Ravensworth by Robert Scott Hopper who purchased the lease from builders Thomas John Jamieson Bell and George Ellison in 1874. The land covered an area of 2,427 square yards being 94' 6" along the east side, which later became Saltwell Road South, by 235' on the north side, 98' 7" along the west side, which later became Breckenbeds Road, and 217' on the south side.

Mayfield Villa (shown as C on the 1895 Ordnance Survey map on the previous page) and its neighbour Westover are located on Saltwell Road South, and was one of the set of four semi-detached properties designed in 1874 by architect William Lister Newcombe. The trade directories and census records note a number of people living at Mayfield or Mayfield Villas. It appears that a few of the houses built along Saltwell Road South by Hopper were named Mayfield, some of which may have been split into apartments. One of the earliest occupiers of Mayfield was Charles Frederick Wormald who was elected a member to the North of England Institute of Mining and Mechanical Engineers on 8 December 1885. The house Wormald occupied was also referred to as number 5 Mayfield Villas.

The 1891 census lists Pierre Alexis Bourgogne, a wine and spirit merchant aged 36, born 1855 in Nuits Saint Georges, France, living at Mayfield with his wife Angelina Emma Broomhead, aged 33 born in 1858, their son Rene Noel Bourgogne, aged 7, daughter Reine Genevieve Bourgogne, aged 4 and one servant. The 1891 census also lists Manuel Rodriguez, a merchant coal exporter aged 40, born in Murcia, Spain and wife Francis Ann Fawcett, aged 40, who were married in Gateshead on 6 December 1879, with their daughter Maria De La Soledad Rodriguez, aged 10, son Fernando Francisco Rodriguez, aged 7, daughter Fanny Rodriguez, aged 7, daughter Elvira Rodriguez, aged 5 and two servants.

In 1918 Charles Frederick Wormald died leaving £16,568 in his will. The trade directory for 1921 shows Mrs Wormald living at Mayfield Villa, then by 1929 Mr J.W. Harvey, a professor, lived there, and in 1935 Mr T.A.H. Rowsell, a bank manager, lived there. The house and the adjoining Westover are now called Westfield Lodge and is split into nine apartments.

Mosscroft

Mosscroft was a two storey house comprising of eight rooms located on Elysium Lane and was the gatehouse at the bottom of the garden of Bensham Grove. The picture below is a copy of a drawing of Mosscroft taken from one of the Mosscroft visitor's books held in Tyne and Wear Archives. The drawing is dated June 1870 and shows two large bay windows to the front elevation and three chimney stacks. The house has ivy climbing up the walls and is surrounded by trees and shrubs. The house was occupied by the Spence Watson family prior to their move into Bensham Grove in 1875 after the death of Joseph Watson.

Image courtesy of Tyne and Wear Archives DF. SPW.

In November 1880 James Pigdon Taylor lived at Mosscroft, who traded with his brother William John Taylor as merchants, ship and insurance brokers, corn factors and ship owners (William John Taylor & Co.). The firm later went into liquidation in 1887. James Pigdon Taylor had already moved from Mosscroft and the 1911 census shows him, aged 61 as a licensed victualler at the Beehive Inn on Belle Vue Bank where he lived with his two daughters in three rooms.

The new occupier of Mosscroft was John Wigham Edmundson who was married to Gertrude Watson, a daughter of Robert Spence Watson of Bensham Grove. In 1883 their son Cyril Edmundson was born at Mosscroft.

By 1887 Mosscroft had another occupier, George Harrison Snowball, a firebrick manufacturer. The firm Snowball Fireclay Products made firebricks, gas retorts (earthenware), tiles and other fire clay goods and was located at Derwenthaugh. The trade directory of 1903 shows Mr Edward H. Richardson of R. Printing Ink Co. Ltd living at Mosscroft. The 1911 census shows Paul Burlando, aged 34, a coal exporter born in Genoa, Italy living at Mosscroft with his Gateshead born wife, Florence, aged 23, son Gigi, aged 5, born in Genoa, son Paul, 18 months born in Gateshead and Marco Rossi, aged 32, a rubber manufacturer born in Italy and two servants.

During the Second World War Mosscroft was a District Emergency Centre with ARP facility.

Below is a poem from one of the Mosscroft visitor's books:

May angels smile on this lovely house

Over its roof tree all blesssings come

Sunshine flit lightly its leaves among

Shadows fall softly its eaves along

Calm may the lives of its dwellers be

Rocked very gently over times rough sea

Oh may they find in thy peace a nest

From the storms and troubles of life to rest

Till they live in Heaven a house more blest.

LC, 2 June 1863

Newe House

Newe House is a four bedroom property situated off Lowreys Lane, Low Fell. The property has private mature gardens with a patio area and two garages.

The photograph below right shows Newe House on Elder Grove. The 1911 census lists Richard Carruthers living at Elderwood on Lowreys Lane, aged 38, with his wife Tilly Agnes, aged 33, sons John, aged 14, James, aged 12, Richard, aged 5 and daughter Elizabeth Tilly, aged 2 years. This suggests the house may have been called Elderwood and changed its name to Newe House or that Newe House was built on the site of a house called Elderwood.

Richard Carruthers had a shop at 580 Durham Road, Low Fell from the turn of the century and was a cabinet maker. He made money during the First World War making hospital beds. One of his sons Richard opened a saw mill at Lamesley. The photograph below shows Richard Carruthers and three of his sons outside the shop in 1928.

Image courtesy of owner.

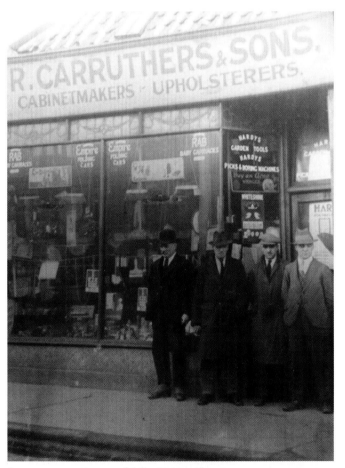

Image courtesy of Mr Carruthers.

An article in the London Gazette on the 29 September 1939:

RICHARD CARRUTHERS Deceased Pursuant to the Trustees Act, 1925

All persons having any claims against the estate of Richard Carruthers, late of Newe House, Lowreys Lane, Low Fell, Gateshead in the county of Durham, Cabinet Maker, Hardware Dealer and Saw Mill Proprietor (who died there on 14th day of March 1939, and whose Will was proved in the Durham District Probate Registry on the 9th day of September 1939, by John Balfour Carruthers, James Carruthers, Richard Carruthers and Stanley Carruthers, the executors therein named), are hereby required to send particulars thereof to us, the undersigned, on or before the 1st day of December 1939, after which date the executors will proceed to distribute the said estate, having regard only to the claims then notified.

Dated the 26th day of September 1939.

H. and A. Swinburne, 12 West Street, Gateshead 8, Solicitors for the said Executors.

The land registry dated 19 April 1961 between Mary Ellen Carruthers and Christopher Carruthers (Vendors) and Harry Dixon and Christine Pelagie Dixon (Purchasers) refers to a right of entry to the adjoining properties to the north of Newe House. Harry Dixon owned Dixon's chemist shop on Beaconsfield Road for many years, and the house was known as the 'Chemist's House'.

North Dene House

North Dene was built in the neo classical style for Richard Hodgson in 1853 where he resided until his death on 26 May 1885. The house, with its impressive stone entrance porch to the main door, had fifteen rooms and was surrounded by gardens with a balustrade to the west looking out towards the Ravensworth Estate.

Image courtesy of Mark Smiles.

The 1901 census lists Arthur Henry Thew living at North Dene with his grandfather Joseph Thompson, a coal owner. An article in the Alnwick Mercury on 23 November 1912 announced the marriage of Arthur H. Thew, the eldest son of A.H. Thew, to Princess Marie Dolgoronky, daughter of the late Prince Michal Michelovitch Dolgoronkov at L'Eglise St. Katherine, Ecole de Droit, St Petersburgh on 18 November 1912, by the Rev. Vicar Vinagradoff.

From September 1953 until the early 1960s the building was used as an annex to Gateshead Grammar School and was later used as part of Gateshead Technical College on Durham Road. North Dene now stands empty within the former Gateshead College grounds, the whole site being owned by Miller Homes.

Whilst a lot of demolition and building work has taken place on the former Gateshead College site unfortunately there have been no alterations or renovations to North Dene since 2012. In August 2015 the site was advertised for sale as an excellent opportunity for development with planning permission for the conversion of North Dene House into seven apartments with nine new build houses in the grounds of the 1.4 acre site (0.58 hectares).

Pallinsburn

Image courtesy of owner.

Pallinsburn is located on Durham Road just south of Aldersyde and Musgrave. The house is a substantial symmetric red brick building with a large bay window at either side of the wide front door. It was built in 1908 for Robert Hogg Clayton, a wealthy businessman. Set to the rear aspect is the garage block which was built at the same time as the main residence to house a coach and horses, with living accommodation on the first floor for the coachman/groom which can be seen in the photograph left.

The 1911 census shows Robert Hogg Clayton, aged 76, a bone-setter, with his second wife Isabella, aged 52, son Robert Hall Clayton, aged 34 and sister-in-law Mary Ingles, aged 55, living at Pallinsburn.

The obituary for Robert H. Clayton from the Newcastle Daily Journal, 22nd January 1916:

Mr Robert H. Clayton of Gateshead, who was well known as a bone-setter on Tyneside, has passed away in his 82nd year. Born at Felling shore in 1834, he commenced work in a coal mine at the age of 7. As a boy, he devoted a great deal of attention to the study of anatomy. His chief mining work was done at Wardley Colliery, where his services in case of injuries were requisitioned by the workmen, and so much was his work appreciated that Dr McLaren, the colliery doctor, asked the owners of the colliery to allow Robert Clayton to render first aid in the doctor's absence – a request which was readily granted. In appreciation of his work of rendering first aid, the officials and workmen of Wardley Colliery presented to Mr Clayton a gold watch in 1874. He left Wardley and commenced as a bone-setter at Felling where he continued to practice until 1908 when he moved to Pallinsburn, Gateshead. He leaves a widow, three sons and five daughters.

Mrs Isabella Clayton continued to live at Pallinsburn after Robert's death, then by 1935 the Misses E. and M.J. Elliott of Musgrave School lived at Pallinsburn. The property was at one time an extension to Musgrave School and between the 1950s and 1970s was the Rectory for St Mary's Parish Church, Gateshead.

Pianet House

The Pianet, later named Pianet House, was situated next to the Magpie public house on Pianet Lane which later became Derwentwater Road, and is now the exit slip road off the A1 at Teams going north. The Pianet can be seen on the 1857 Ordnance Survey map below but is not named on the 1951 Ordnance Survey map.

Reproduced with Permission. Ordnance Survey.

The 1851 census shows the Ivison family living at Pianet, William Ivison and his wife Sarah formerly Dailey, with son David and daughters Mary and Catherine who was born c. 1850.

Redheugh Villa

Redheugh Villa was located just off Duke Street near to Team Street and can be seen on the photograph below to the right of the single gas storage tank. The building was still there until the late 1970s or early 80s. The area is now grass and trees at the junction of Team Street and Autumn Road.

Image courtesy of Newcastle City Library.

In 1876 a new gas works opened at Redheugh. The earliest mention of Redheugh Villa in the trade directories is in 1883 which lists Mr Robert Moody, a manager at the gas works living there. Mr Moody is listed in the trade directories to around 1894.

Redheugh Villa must have been used for gas works staff as the house was well located amongst the gas works buildings and silos.

The trade directories for 1903 to 1906 show Mr George Henderson, an assistant manager for the gas works living at Redheugh Villa. The 1925 trade directory shows Mr F.H. Vince, works superintendent, and Mr J. Dobson, a foreman at Redheugh Villa, then by 1929 Mr A.H. Gibson, was the works superintendent and Mr J. Dobson, the foreman.

Saltwell Vale House

Saltwell Vale House was located on Durham Road, Low Fell, near the top of Albert Drive where the shops are set back from Durham Road. The house would have had an elevated position with spectacular views across the Ravensworth Estate.

There was a large stone columned porch entrance and large bay windows to the south and west sides of the house. The garden was laid out to lawn with shrubs, trees and planters, and a number of garden seats were located on the west side of the house to enjoy the view.

In 1837 it was the home of Robert Robson whose daughter, Mary Robson born c. 1804, married Thomas Sowerby on Monday, 7 December 1835 at St John's Church. Thomas was born in 1790 at Netherton Farm, Cumberland and was the seventh child, fourth son of John and Abigail Sowerby. By 1841 Thomas and Mary were living at Saltwell Vale. They had six children. Their first daughter Mary Josephine (nicknamed Demmie) married Christian Rudolph Fernando Thiedemann on Wednesday 26 October 1859 and later moved to The Cedars.

Their second daughter, Elizabeth, had died in infancy at Belle Vue House and was buried 15 December 1837. Their third daughter, Catherine, also died in infancy, 2 days old in 1838. In 1840 their son Thomas was born but sadly died on Tuesday, 11 April 1843, aged 2 years. Their fourth daughter, Catherine (known as Kate), was born c. 1842 and married George Highfield, a farmer, who lived at Blencogo near Wigton, Cumbria. Their youngest child Martha was born in 1844, then just three years later on Sunday, 20 June 1847 Thomas's wife Mary died, aged 43.

Thomas was business partner with John Phillips who was married to his sister Elizabeth. Between 1850 and 1860 Thomas and Phillips became owners of Chester Moor South Colliery, and in 1855 the ownership of Waldridge Colliery passed to Thomas Sowerby. Thomas was nominated as a candidate for election as councillor of the South Ward of the Borough in November 1841, and became an Alderman in 1843, he retired from the council in 1844. In 1846 he was elected a member of the Royal Agricultural Society of England, and was also director of Tyne Marine Insurance Company.

Thomas died at Saltwell Vale House on Wednesday, 18 March 1863, aged 73, then his daughter Catherine, who had come to nurse him, died on Tuesday, 14 April 1863, aged 20 of scarlatina (Scarlet Fever). After her father's death, Martha went to live with her sister Mary Thiedemann and on Wednesday, 27 December 1865, married George John Bennett at St Paul's, Elswick.

Thomas had made his will on 13 March 1863, just five days before he died. He was buried at St John's Church, Gateshead on Saturday, 21 March 1863. On his death the house and furniture was put up for auction. An article in the Newcastle Courant on Friday, 3 April 1863 advertised the sale of Saltwell Vale, and articles in the Newcastle Courant on Friday, 8 and 15 May 1863 announced the sale of the furniture, and the crops were sold off in August 1863.

Saltwell Vale House is shown on the 1857 Ordnance Survey Map below.

Reproduced with Permission. Ordnance Survey.

The 1868 Mercer & Crockett's directory shows Mr G. Elliott living at Saltwell Vale, then the Christies Directory for 1870 shows Mr George Miller, a hat manufacturer. The 1873 to 1880 trade directories show Thomas Sowerby's youngest daughter, Martha Bennett, described as a Lady, living at Saltwell Vale House.

The 1881 census lists Mary Stark, a 48 year old widow living at Saltwell Vale House. She is described as an annuitant born in Gainsborough, Lincolnshire, and lived with her son and daughter, a visitor and one servant. The 1891 census shows Francis William Haggie, aged 39, a rope manufacturer, living there with his wife Frances, aged 36. Francis William Haggie was born in Gateshead in June 1852, the second son of Peter and Elizabeth Haggie. Francis William married Frances Tarbuck and had one son, Francis Reginald Haggie.

The photograph right was taken in the grounds of Saltwell Vale House around 1898 and shows a group of men learning first aid. The owner of Saltwell Vale was John Adolphus Harrison who was superintendent of Gateshead Fell division of the St John Ambulance Brigade. The 1901 census describes John Adolphus Harrison, aged 58, as a coal exporter and ship owner living at the house with his wife Lucy, aged 54, and daughter Mary Elizabeth, aged 24, and servants. John Adolphus Harrison died on 30 April 1902, aged 59, leaving

Image courtesy of Beamish Museum Archives.

£20,385 4s 1d. Probate was granted to John F. Fenwick, a shipowner, Philip Edward Mather, a solicitor and Lucy Harrison, his widow.

The 1905/06 trade directory shows Mr J.W. Frazer, an architect, living at Saltwell Vale House. The 1918 directory shows J. Creigh, a buyer, and the 1925 directory shows Mr J. Phillips, a draper, then the 1937 to 1939 trade directories show Saltwell Vale House as Low Fell Preparatory School. During the Second World War, Saltwell Vale House was used as a District Emergency Centre with ARP facility.

Sandmill House

Sandmill House is situated on Windy Nook Road, Sheriff Hill. The house is a double fronted rough stone building with a slate roof, stone lintels above the windows and has the name Sandmill House on the porch. Sandmill House was built in the early 19th century.

An article in the Newcastle Journal on 2 October 1858 recorded the sale of four closes of land, with the farm buildings, sand mill, joiner's shop and other erections thereon, now in the occupation of John Bullerwell a farmer of 12 acres of land, John Hunter and John Hill, and delightfully situated in Gateshead High Fell.

The 1861 census shows Isabella Bullerwell (wife of John Bullerwell), aged 39, originally from Gosforth, living at Sandmill House. She is described as the head of the household. Living with her were her daughter Frances, aged 12, son George, aged 10, daughter Sarah Isabella, aged 7, daughter Mary Ann, aged 4 and baby son John Thomas. Also living with the family was her mother-in-law Frances, aged 79.

Image used courtesy of owner.

South Dene

South Dene is situated on Sidmouth Road off Chowdene Bank and is a semi-detached property with Dene House. On the Ordnance Survey map of 1894, Dene House and South Dene look as though they could be one large property. Then by the 1919 Ordnance Survey map they show distinctly as two separate properties. The photograph right shows the recently renovated house with beautiful stone bay windows to the west elevation looking out over the Team Valley, and stone steps leading to a large porch entrance.

Image used courtesy of owner.

The 1879 trade directory shows Henry and Thomas Hedley living at South Dene. It is not clear whether the two brothers were living in the same house or the name of the house was incorrectly recorded for Thomas. The 1883/84 trade directory only lists Henry living at South Dene. (Thomas is recorded as living at Dene House.) Henry was born in 1841, the youngest son of Thomas and Susan Hedley both of Northumberland. Henry had three older brothers, James, John and Thomas.

Painting used courtesy of owner.

Henry died around 1901, as the trade directory for that year only shows Mrs Henry Hedley living at South Dene. On his death he left £10,084 9s 2d; probate was granted to James Dodds Hedley and his widow Jane Anne.

Then the trade directories of 1903 to 1918 show Mr Charles Humble, a chartered accountant of 12 West Street, residing at South Dene. The 1925 to 1939 trade directories show Mr F.W. Vaughan, a managing director living there. Mr Vaughan owned a yellow Rolls Royce which he loaned out to Gateshead Corporation to transport visiting dignitaries.

The painting left of South Dene has been handed down from owner to owner.

South Dene Tower

The beautiful castellated building in red and white brick was bought by John Marriner Redmayne in 1865 for £12,500. John Marriner Redmayne was born in 1831 in Middlesex and, with his older brother Robert Robey Redmayne, were directors of Felling Chemical Co. and, with another director Hugh Lee Pattinson, were responsible for the erection of Christ Church in Felling.

John's son Sir Richard Augustine Studdert Redmayne became Chief Inspector of Mines and was a mining expert conducting many inquiries into mining disasters. He was invested as a Knight in 1914, and was President of The Institute of Professional Civil Servants between 1922 and 1955. Sir Richard Augustine Studdert Redmayne is the great-grandfather of the actor Edward John David Redmayne who played Stephen Hawking in 'The Theory of Everything' for which he won the Academy Award, BAFTA Award, Golden Globe Award and the Screen Actors Guild Award.

An article in the Newcastle Daily Journal on 29 December 1915 announced the engagement of the Marquis of Granby, the only son of the Duke and Duchess of Rutland, and Miss Kathleen Tennant, youngest daughter of Mr and Mrs Frank Tennant of Innes House, Morayshire. Miss Tennant's mother was the daughter of the late John Marriner Redmayne, whose family had been closely identified with the industrial development of Tyneside, and a niece of the Prime Minister Herbert Asquith and Mrs Asquith. Her father, Mr Francis John Tennant the second surviving son of the late Sir Charles Tennant, Bart., was for several years, a familiar figure in the House of Commons.

Image courtesy of Gateshead Library Archives.

During the Second World War, South Dene Tower was an ARP Report and Control Centre and an Auxiliary Fire Service Station. The entrance to an old air raid shelter was located near the south east of the grounds and was visible for many years from East Park Road.

South Dene Tower was the model for Saltwell Towers and was demolished in 1956; the Crematorium and grounds now occupy the site.

Springfield House

Springfield House was built around the 1880s by Alderman George Hornsby Dexter, a timber merchant and former Mayor of Jarrow. The 1891 census shows Dexter living there with his daughter Florence, aged 25, son Tom, aged 23 a gardener, son Jesse, aged 20 a clerk, daughters Mary A.J., aged 18, Fanny P., aged 17 a scholar, son George, aged 11 a scholar, a cousin Mary Ilderton, aged 47 and servant Maria Boyd, aged 25 years.

The photograph below taken in 1948 of the residential area surrounding Deckham and Shipcote, shows Springfield House (marked A below) to the far right of the Springfield Hotel near the corner of Dryden Road. Springfield House was later demolished when the hotel was extended. The house to the south is Lindum House (marked B below).

A – Springfield House. B – Lindum House. Image © Historic England. Licensor canmore.org.uk.

One of the most notable owners of Springfield House was Sir John Maccoy who in September 1917 received notification that his son, Lance-Corporal Percy Maccoy of the Canadian Scottish, had been killed in action. Percy Maccoy had emigrated to Canada at the age of 19. He had joined the Canadian Overseas Expeditionary Force on 11 April 1916 and died on 13 September 1917 in trenches north west of Angres. Lance-Corporal Maccoy was aged 31.

Sir John was formerly Superintendent of the Prince Line of steamers, had completed thirty years' service on Gateshead Borough Council, was eight times Mayor of Gateshead and Knighted in 1922. In 1930 Sir John Maccoy donated three stained glass windows to Gateshead Town Hall (right).

Image courtesy of Gateshead Library Archives.

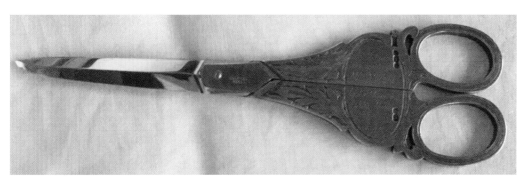

At the unveiling ceremony for the windows, a ribbon was cut with a pair of silver scissors, shown left.

Images courtesy of Ms H. Crick.

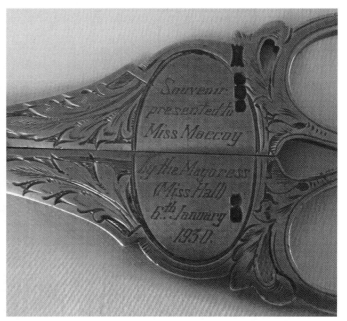

The engraving on the scissors (above left) reads: '*Unveiling of Stained Glass Windows in the Council Chamber, Gateshead, the gift of Ald Sir John Maccoy DL to the Corporation*'. The reverse side (above right) reads: '*Souvenir presented to Miss Maccoy by the Mayoress (Miss Hall) 6th January 1930.*'

The scissors were passed down from Miss Maccoy and are now owned by one of Sir John Maccoy's great-granddaughters who kindly provided these images.

Stirling House

Stirling House was originally built in the late 19th century as a residence for John Ross the builder and would have had a pleasant view over the Team Valley.

The trade directory for 1897/98 shows John Ross, a builder with premises on Elysium Lane, resident on Saltwell Road. John Ross was born in Newcastle around 1856 and was a house builder. The trade directory for 1901/02 describes him as an auctioneer, valuer and fire loss adjuster with premises at 44 Brunswick Terrace. Ross had previously lived at Bensham Hall Lodge, which was the lodge for Bensham Hall and was located on Saltwell Lane very close to the site that Stirling House was built. It is not clear whether the lodge was extended to become Stirling House, or Stirling House was built alongside.

An article from the Newcastle Courant dated 1898, recorded:

> Gateshead Municipal Elections
>
> John Ross, Auctioneer and Builder of Stirling House
> has consented to offer himself for North West Council Seat.
>
> Saturday, 8 October 1898

Postcard series: Gibson of Gateshead.

The area changed dramatically in the early 20th century as rows of Tyneside flats were built which can be seen from the postcard above of Saltwell Road showing Stirling House situated close to the roadside with terraced shops and houses on each side. John Ross built many of the streets in the area including Dunsmuir Grove and Kelvin Grove.

Stirling House was a two storeyed building with attic rooms and had five windows across the front and an impressive stone entrance. The house is now known as the Stirling House public house located at 173 Saltwell Road on the corner of Dunsmuir Grove.

Image used courtesy of owner.

In later years the building was extended to the north at the front elevation and to the rear, possibly at the time it became a public house in order to add more function rooms and accommodation.

Team Lodge

Team Lodge was shown on the 1856 Ordnance Survey map, and can be seen on the 1895 Ordnance Survey map below which shows its location off Saltwell Road near South Dene Tower and was there until the late 1890s.

The Ward's Directory for 1869 lists Thomas Longridge Gooch living at Team Lodge. The 1871 census shows Thomas Longridge Gooch, aged 62, and his wife Ruthanna, aged 57, from Newcastle living at Team Lodge with four servants. Thomas Longridge Gooch was born in Brompton, London in November 1808, the eldest son of John Gooch of Bedlington and Anna, daughter of Thomas Longridge of Newcastle.

Gooch had been an apprentice to George Stephenson and had surveyed the Newcastle and Carlisle Railway from 1826 with Stephenson. Gooch acted as Stephenson's secretary and draughtsman on the Liverpool and Manchester Railway and lived in Stephenson's house in Liverpool.

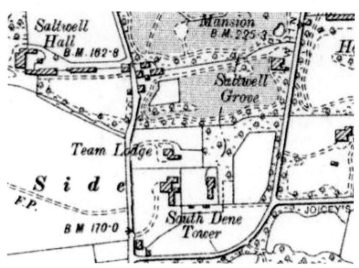

Reproduced with Permission. Ordnance Survey.

In January 1829, Gooch became Resident Engineer for the Liverpool end of the Liverpool and Manchester Railway and, in April the same year, he took a temporary appointment as resident engineer of the Bolton and Leigh Railway.

Stephenson was appointed to survey the route of the proposed Manchester and Leeds Railway in 1830 and Gooch was appointed his assistant. Gooch was the civil engineer for the Manchester and Leeds Railway from 1831 to 1844.

In 1861 his daughter Mary married Robert Robey Redmayne. Redmayne with his younger brother John Marriner Redmayne were directors of Felling Chemical Co. Thomas Longridge Gooch died on 23 November 1882. His wife Ruthanna continued to live at Team Lodge until 1890 then, by 1897/98, the trade directory shows Mr H. Eastcott, an engineer, living there.

The Cedars

The Cedars was situated on Ivy Lane off Durham Road, Low Fell. The 1874 to 1886 trade directories show Mr Christian Rudolph Fernando Thiedemann, a merchant and ship broker, living at The Cedars. Thiedemann was born in Eckemforde, Denmark c. 1825 (Schleswig, Germany). Thiedemann gained nationalisation on 11 October 1856. He married Mary Sowerby, daughter of Thomas and Mary Sowerby of Saltwell Vale House, Low Fell on 26 October 1859 at the Parish Church on Gateshead Fell.

Before living at The Cedars the 1861 census shows Thiedemann, aged 34, living at 24 Rye Hill, Newcastle, a merchant's importer of grains and Baltic produce, exporter of coal and Baltic products to Europe. Christian and Mary had a son, Thomas Edward born 1861, a son Rudolph born 1863 and daughters Kate born 1865 and Mary born in 1869.

The census for 1871 describes Thiedemann as a ship owner and colliery owner employing hundreds of men. Thiedemann held a 28 year lease with John Joicey and others of Waldridge Colliery around 1872.

After moving to The Cedars, their son Rudolph died in June 1875, aged 12 years, and in 1876 Christian and Mary had another daughter Eliza. The 1881 census shows the family at The Cedars; Christian is aged 55 and described as a Foreign Merchant, shipowner and colliery owner. On 15 May 1882 his wife Mary died at The Cedars; the Probate showed she left £41,296 6s 6d. A few years later, in 1888, their son Thomas Edward Thiedemann died on 25 March at The Cedars leaving £4,014 2s 3d. Christian died on 14 March 1890 at The Cedars, leaving £31,612 11s 6d.

Jesmond Cemetery record:

The family burial place of Christian Rudolph Fernando Thiedemann of The Cedars, Eighton Banks, Lamesley. Rudolph Thiedemann their son who died 9th June 1875, aged 12 years. CHRISTIAN RUDOLPH FERNANDO THIEDEMANN died March 14th 1890 aged 64 years. Mary wife of Christian Rudolph Fernando Thiedemann died May 6th 1882 aged 46 years. Their first son Thomas Edward Thiedemann born October 15th 1860 died March 25th 1888.

The Cedars is shown near Fellside House on the 1895 Ordnance Survey map right.

The 1891 census shows another family living at The Cedars. Bessie White, aged 70, widow of John White, a gentleman shipowner, who had previously lived at 11 Ogle Terrace, South Shields. John was one of the original town councillors in South Shields in

Reproduced with Permission. Ordnance Survey.

1850. Bessie was living with her daughter Ann Lee, aged 47, her son John, aged 45 a shipbroker, son Edwin, aged 40 a solicitor, daughters Marian, aged 36, Julianna, aged 34, Edith S., aged 32, Sarah G., aged 30 and four servants.

By the 1911 census her son John White, aged 66 is now head of the household, a steam tug owner with his sisters Anna Lee, aged 67, Marian E., aged 56, Julianna, aged 54 and Edith, aged 52. Then the 1921 to 1939 trade directories show Mr Harry Noble, an engineer, living at The Cedars.

By the 1960s much of the grounds of The Cedars had been sold off and Cedars Green housing estate was built. The house was then owned by Gateshead Council and became a school for physically disabled children for many years. The house was demolished in the late 1980s or early 1990s and new houses built on the site.

The Croft

The Croft is situated on Springwell Road, Wrekenton. The house is a large stone property with bay windows to the ground floor, and can first be seen on the 1919 to 1926 Ordnance survey map located a little west of Wrekenton House.

It would seem that The Croft was built as a surgery for Wrekenton as the trade directory for 1905 shows Mr James Law, a surgeon aged 44, born in Lancashire, living there with his wife Eveline May Crawford, aged 23. Eveline May died in 1908, aged 26. The 1911 census shows Mr James Law, aged 51, a widowed medical practitioner and a Mr John Vincent Grant, aged 27 from Inverness, a medical practitioner, and two staff living at The Croft. James Law later moved to Ayton House, Wrekenton and died on 17 April 1943; he left £33,427 0s 5d to Thomas Crawford a retired mining engineer. The later trade directory of 1937 shows Mr R.J. McMullan, a surgeon, living at The Croft.

Today the building is occupied by the NHS service.

Drawing by W.H. Wake 1975.

The Datcha

The Datcha is situated on Alverstone Avenue, Low Fell. The semi-detached house was built around 1908 in an art-deco style, partially rendered with a rosemary-tiled roof, highly symmetrical in design.

The 1911 census records Dixon Scott a theatre proprietor living at The Datcha with his wife and children. Dixon Scott was the great-uncle of Hollywood directors Sir Ridley Scott, director of 'Gladiator', 'Alien', 'Kingdom of Heaven' and 'Prometheus' fame, and the late Tony Scott,

Image used courtesy of owner.

director of 'Top Gun', 'Days of Thunder', 'Crimson Tide' and 'True Romance'.

Dixon Scott (below) was a local film entrepreneur who built the Tyneside Cinema in Newcastle which opened as the 'Newcastle News Theatre' on 1 February 1937. Scott's travels to the Middle and Far East influenced the décor for the inside of the Theatre, with gold, green and purple; some of these features were brought back to life when the Cinema was restored in 2008. Dixon Scott died in 1939 and is buried in Cairo.

The house is now called Tyne Holme.

Image courtesy of the Tyneside Cinema.

The photograph right shows the beautiful art-deco windows around the front door.

Image used courtesy of owner.

The Gables

The Gables is situated at number 669 Durham Road, Low Fell attached at right angles to Victoria Place which was built in 1840, so the house is aptly named being on the gable end.

The house was built of stone from the nearby quarry, which was located where Low Fell park is today, by colliery manager Mr Steele; and was at that time one house with the attached number 667. Steele had previously built Home House on Kells Lane in the 1820s.

The entrance gate off Durham Road leads you through a pretty garden to the front of the house which has a single storey and a two storey bay window together with a portico to the front door. The house had a stable block to the rear which has since been rebuilt as a double garage. The photograph left shows the

Image used courtesy of owner of number 667 Durham Road.

drainage grooves in the original stone and brick flooring.

The 1911 census shows Mr James Muir Nelson Paton, aged 40, a medical practitioner born in Troon, South Ayrshire, with his wife Gertrude Dora, aged 31, their daughter Dorothy Margaret, aged 4, his mother-in-law Dorothy Payne, aged 56 and one servant living at The Gables. The trade directory for 1913/14 also shows Mr J.M. Paton referred to as a physician living at The Gables. In January 1916 in aid of the funds for the Gateshead Fell St John Nursing Division Mrs Paton gave a very successful whist drive at The Gables. The sum of £8 11s was raised by Mrs Paton's effort.

Image used courtesy of owner.

A later resident recorded in a newspaper article in the Northern Daily Mail dated 18 November 1927 noted:

Mr H.A. Haslam, liberal candidate for the Seaham Division, is again laid up with illness at his home The Gables, Low Fell, Gateshead, and it is feared he will be unable to take any further part in the contest.

Later residents were the Moon family and Mrs Moon was known to have garden parties to raise funds for the Chapel opposite the house on Durham Road. In 1936 the house was split into two dwellings by the Moon brothers, the northerly property was named Glendale (now number 667) and the southerly property remained The Gables. The Gables now has an attractive arched alcove at the far end of the hallway on both the ground and first floors which were passageways of the original house before it was separated into two properties.

The Moon brothers were partners in the Beacon Garage (left) a short distance from the house, now a Kwik Fit Garage.

Image courtesy of Gateshead Library Archives.

The house stood on a very large plot with a large garden area; part of this area was sold off in the 1980s and a dwelling off Kells Lane was later built. The Gables was added to the Council's list of Buildings of Special Local Architectural or Historic Interest in 2004.

Image used courtesy of owner.

The Hermitage

The Hermitage was a mansion with twenty rooms and was built in 1870 for Mr John Cotes Copland. Around 1915 Robert Bales Armstrong lived at The Hermitage with his family of eight children. The photograph below shows the family in 1916 relaxing outside the front of the house.

Robert Bales Armstrong was born in West Herrington, and came from a very ordinary sheep-farming family that originated from Slaggyford near Alston. He became a marine engineer/architect and worked at Hawthorn Leslie shipyards on the Tyne. He was awarded an OBE in 1918 for his part in keeping the shipyards open during the First World War. He became managing director of R. & W. Hawthorn, Leslie and Co. Ltd, but unfortunately died three months later in 1931.

Image courtesy of Mrs S. Butcher.

This family group photograph taken c. 1916 shows Robert Bales Armstrong seated with his wife Margaret Emma. Standing behind are two of their sons in army uniform, John, aged 20 on the left and Rob, aged 22 on the right, the two young ladies in front are their fiancées. Their older son Frank, aged 23, had died in the war in 1915. Their two daughters sitting in front are Doris Hunter Armstrong on the left and her younger sister Gladys on the right.

Below the girls are having afternoon tea at the front of the house.

Images courtesy of Mrs S. Butcher.

The house had lovely gardens with 'dells' and the photograph above shows the family on the lawn surrounded by trees and shrubs.

The summer house at the end of the bridge grew camellias and grapes.

By 1920 The Hermitage had become the High Fell Working Men's Institute before the club moved to modern premises on Old Durham Road. The Hermitage was demolished about 1964.

Wellwood

The land on Saltwell Road South near Station Road that Wellwood was built on was leased from Lord Ravensworth on 1 May 1874 to Thomas John Jamieson Bell and George Ellison (builders) who secured the leasehold of two pieces of land with the power to erect eight semi-detached villas.

On 11 July 1874 the builders T.J.J. Bell and G. Ellison agreed the sale and mortgaged the leased land to Robert Scott Hopper, a gentleman solicitor of Newcastle. Before they had erected and finished two of the semi-detached villas on one of the pieces of ground, T.J.J. Bell and G. Ellison contracted with Robert Scott Hopper to sell him the two semi-detached villas and all their estate for the sum of £3,000. By the end of 1874 Robert Scott Hopper was the occupant of the most northerly of the villas, which would later be known as Wellwood.

Image used courtesy of owner.

Robert Scott Hopper then completed the remaining six semi-detached villas and other buildings. Hopper deposited the title deeds with Hodgkin Barnett & Co. on 3 September 1883 for securing the repayment on demand of certain moneys. The bank later requested payment of the money owing but Hopper was unable to pay, the bank required him to give them the securities for the payment of £5,953 10s 4d, being the amount then due and interest of £15 13s 4d making a sum of £5,969 3s 8d.

On 12 November 1884 Robert Scott Hopper agreed a mortgage payment with Thomas Hodgkin and John William Pease, Bankers, who were two of the partners of the firm Hodgkin Barnett & Co. The payment was to be paid in equal half yearly payments but on 19 November 1885 a writ of summons was issued in action between Hodgkin Barnett & Co. and Robert Scott Hopper, claiming Hopper should be foreclosed of his equity of redemption of the mortgage dated 12 November 1884. Hodgkin Barnett & Co. extended the deadline in 1887, Hopper then owed £6,645 12s 6d. Hopper foreclosed on mortgage and equity in 1888, and the firm of Hodgkin Barnett Pease Spence & Co. became the new owners of the land, property and Title Deeds. The 1891 census shows Hopper living at Eslington Villas and then by 1911 he is living in Whitley Bay.

On 25 March 1907 John William Pease died and the Title Deeds changed on 5 November 1907 between the Right Honourable Arthur Thomas Baron Ravensworth (first part), Sir Hedworth Williamson, the Honourable Archibald Dudley Ryder (second part) and James Arnott Sisson (third part). Due to the 'settled Land Act 1882-1890' Arthur Thomas Baron Ravensworth sold the ownership of the land to James Arnott Sisson, who continued the leaseholds on the villas.

On 6 November 1907, James Arnott Sisson Esq, Chartered Accountant of Hillcroft, sold Wellwood to Allison Sutherland Bell who had leased the house for many years. The land covered an area of 2,453 square yards being 111' 3" along the east side, which later became Saltwell Road South, by 186' along the north side, 120' along the west side and 196' 6" along the south side. Also included was a small plot of land between Station Road and Breckenbeds Road referred to as a detached garden belonging to Wellwood on the left of the drawing right.

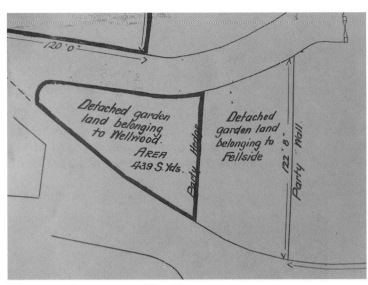

Plan used courtesy of owner.

The house is approached via a long curved driveway leading up to the front of the house which has two storeys, attic rooms and cellar; and retains the original sash windows. On the first floor there is a hidden door that would have led into Glenside house at one time and may have been for servants to move from one house to the other or created for Allison Sutherland Bell to call upon her younger sister Isabella who was married to John Archibald Dixon of Glenside. Allison Bell sold the house to Mr John William Rounthwaite, an architect of 26 Saltwell View, in September 1911. Rounthwaite died in February 1927 and in August 1927 his estate was sold to Swinburne Wilson Newton, a seed merchant, and his wife Isabella. Isabella died on 27 July 1963, aged 83 and Swinburne died on 14 May 1964, aged 85. Both Isabella and Swinburne are buried at Lamesley. Newton's Estate sold Wellwood in December 1964. The house was then sold in May 1967 and August 1970 then again in 1982 to the present owners from Mr and Mrs Frank Atkinson. Frank Atkinson had been the creator of Beamish Open-Air Museum.

Westover

Westover was also built on land leased from Lord Ravensworth by Robert Scott Hopper who purchased the lease from builders Thomas John Jamieson Bell and George Ellison in 1874.

The land covered an area of 2,391 square yards being 100' 4" along the east side, which later became Saltwell Road South, by 217' on the north side 103' along the west side, which later became Breckenbeds Road and 207' 6" along the south side.

Westover (shown as B on the 1895 map left) and its semi-detached Mayfield neighbour are located on Saltwell Road South just south of Hillcroft North and Hillcroft South. The trade directory from 1885 lists Mr Richard Price, a bank manager, living there. The 1891 census shows Price, aged 63, with his wife Elenor, aged 74, son Anthony, aged 34, daughters Gertrude, aged 32, and Marian, aged 27, sister-in-law Mary Ann Simon, aged 75 and two servants.

A later resident in 1896 was Edward Carrick Watson, the son of William Wigham and Mary Watson, born in Gateshead 27 December 1841.

Watson was in business as a land surveyor by 1869 and married Alice Brady at Barnsley in 1872. He had acted as agent with his cousin Robert Spence Watson for Albert Grey in the South Northumberland election in 1880. Watson later moved to 5 Carlton Terrace, Low Fell, where he died on 5 November 1929, leaving £4,848 5s 0d.

Westover and the adjoining Mayfield Villa are now known as Westfield Lodge and are split into nine apartments.

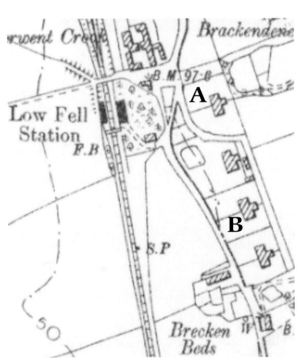

A – Wellwood. B – Westover.
Reproduced with Permission. Ordnance Survey

Whinney House

Whinney House, situated off Durham Road, Low Fell, was built around 1865 for John and Edward Joicey, coal owners, and has been a Grade II listed building since 13 January 1983.

Whinney House became a convalescent hospital for wounded soldiers in 1915. The postcard below shows nurses and soldiers outside the conservatory.

Private collection.

Below is an image of a nurse's pin badge showing the letters 'W' and 'H' for Whinney House. The service ceased in 1919.

Private collection.

In 1921 the house and grounds were purchased by Gateshead Corporation and served as a hospital, initially for tuberculosis sufferers and later for old people. Whinney House was used as a Decontamination, Rescue and Repair Depot during the Second World War. In 1974 it was transferred from Gateshead Corporation to Gateshead Health Authority. The house then served as an administrative base and a centre for people with learning disabilities, and was later purchased by the Jewish Community for Torah studies.

The image below shows a rotary hut at Whinney House which was used for open-air treatment. The rotary hut was considered the most up-to date equipment.

Private collection.

Image courtesy of Bob Dixon.

In 2012 Whinney House was purchased by the company Saltwell Park Developments, at which point it had planning permission to convert the building into fifteen apartments. Saltwell Park Developments amended the planning to create five houses and six apartments as this was a lot more sympathetic to the building. The restoration and conversion started in 2013 and was completed in 2015. The photograph above shows the rear of Whinney House and the beautiful fountain as it is today.

Woodlands (Brackendene)

Woodlands is located on Brackendene Drive, Low Fell, near the bottom of Belle Vue Bank. Woodlands is a large two storey building with views over the Team Valley.

The 1911 census shows John Fenwick, aged 45 a coal merchant, living at Woodlands. Also his wife Elizabeth Mary, aged 38, son Frank, aged 11, daughters Nora, aged 7 and Marjorie, aged 3. Also living in the house are Jane Cairns, aged 80, and three servants.

John Fenwick was born on 2 July 1865 in Northumberland, the son of Joseph Fenwick, aged 26

Image courtesy of owner.

and Isabella Stuart Arkless, aged 20. His brother Francis was born 27 November 1866 when Joseph was 1 year old. Their father Joseph died on 7 November 1868 on the Isle of Wight at the age of 29.

Joseph's mother, Isabella Stuart Arkless, died at Woodlands, Brackendene on 7 January 1925, aged 80, when Joseph was 59. His brother Francis died 14 January 1926, and Joseph died 3 May 1937, aged 71, in Ponteland.

The photograph right shows the beautiful stained glass in the hall window.

Image courtesy of owner.

Woodlands (Church Road)

A second house called Woodlands is a stone property situated on the north corner of Church Road, Low Fell opposite the Plantation and was built in 1870. The property has a high stone wall and a large entrance with metal gates and stone pillars.

From the original deeds and outline property plans, the first conveyance took place between William Reed Worley the builder and the buyer Edward Blanch, a butcher of Gateshead High Street, on 17 September 1874 for the princely sum of £110. The plans of the house, which faces west, describes it as being on Meeting House Lane, which changes to Church Road as it turns the corner upwards towards St John's Church. After three years, Mr Blanch sold the house back to the Worley's for £825. The Worley's then sell, on 28 August 1877, to Mrs S.F. Hay and trustee, who on 1 August 1908 sells the house on to James Cawthorn.

James Cawthorn died on 31 March 1910. The 1911 census shows William Medlar living at Woodlands, a railway clerk, aged 54. Also living in the house are his wife Jane, aged 53, their son William Leighton Medlar, aged 26, daughter Jane Cawthorn Medlar, aged 24, son Thomas Cawthorn Medlar, aged 17, son Robert Leighton Medlar, aged 14, and three nieces, Charlotte Cawthorn, aged 22, Florence Elizabeth Cawthorn, aged 20 and Isabella Jane Cawthorn, aged 18.

The 1920 electoral register shows Mr John Innes Mather, a merchant, and Ethel Newton Mather living at Woodlands.

A later conveyance is shown to be between Mr William D. Stackhouse to Mr A. Howard Hall, a civil engineer, in 1931. The present owners bought the house from Mr Hall's widow in 1985.

Image used courtesy of owner.

Acknowledgements

The authors would like to thank: Gateshead Library Archives, Beamish Museum Archives, AAG Archaeology, Historic England, Miller Homes, the NHS, Newcastle City Library, Ordnance Survey, Saltwell Park Development, Tyne and Wear Archives and the Tyneside Cinema.

Thanks also go to Gateshead Local History Society for funding the publication.

We would like to thank the following for their contribution to the book: Sue Bleazard, Mrs S. Butcher, Mr Carruthers, Ms H. Crick, Tom Cruikshank, Mrs J.D. Goddard, Duncan Hall, Glen Hodgins, Anthea Lang, Hugh Mackay, Doreen McNally, Mark Smiles, Mr J. Turnbull, W.H. Wake and our special thanks to Shirley Brown for writing the foreword.

Our thanks also to the owners and occupiers of the following houses who have supported our research and kindly allowed us permission to use a photograph of their property, some of whom have also provided detail and photographs for which we are most grateful: Belle Vue House, Birchholme, Dene House, Eighton Lodge, Field House, Ford House, Glenside, Harewood House, Hill House, Newe House, Pallinsburn, Sandmill House, South Dene, The Stirling public house, The Croft, The Datcha, The Gables, Wellwood, Woodlands (Brackendene) and Woodlands (Church Road).
   Please respect the privacy of these home owners and occupiers.

All other photographs are the copyright of Sandra Brack, Bob Dixon and Helen Ward.

Also thanks to our publisher Andrew Clark.

Whilst every effort has been made to contact and acknowledge due copyright within this book, we would like to thank those copyright holders of any material contained within this publication where this has not been possible.

Springfield House. Image © Historic England. Licensor canmore.org.uk.

Bibliography

Written sources:

Gateshead's Grand Houses – Sandra Brack (Gateshead Local History Society)

Probate index of James Pollock Esq 20 May 1867 (Bensham Cottage)

Probate index of Elizabeth Thomas 8 February 1839 (Bensham Lodge)

An article in the British Medical Journal 14 October 1961 (Bensham Lodge)

An article in the Newcastle Chronicle Saturday 1 August 1770 (Carr Hill House)

19th Battalion Northumberland Fusiliers Roll of Honour (Dene House)

An article in the Sunderland Daily Echo Monday 11 August 1902 (Ford House)

An article in the Yorkshire Post and Leeds Intelligencer 13 May 1903 (Harewood House)

An article in the London Gazette 29 September 1939 (Newe House)

An article in the Alnwick Mercury 23 November 1912 (North Dene)

An article in the Newcastle Daily Journal 22 January 1916 (Pallinsburn)

Articles in the Newcastle Courant Friday 3 April 1863, Friday 8 May 1863 and Friday 15 May 1863 (Saltwell Vale House)

An article in the Newcastle Journal 2 October 1858 (Sandmill House)

An article in the Newcastle Daily Journal 29 December 1915 (South Dene Tower)

An article in the Yorkshire Post and Leeds Intelligencer 27 September 1917 (Springfield House)

An article in the Newcastle Courant 1898 (Stirling House)

An article in the Northern Daily Mail 18 November 1927 (The Gables)

UK Census

Trade Directories

Deeds of: Harewood House, Hill House, Wellwood and Woodlands (Church Road)

Postcard:
Gibson of Gateshead postcard (Stirling House)

Websites:

www.gracesguide.co.uk (Bensham Cottage and Team Lodge)

www.benshamgrove.org.uk (Bensham Grove)

www.westfieldmemorialvillage.co.uk/history-benefactors.htm (Fellside House)

www.mocavo.co.uk/Biographical-History-of-Gonville-and-Caius-College-1349-1897 (Ford House)

www.workhouses.org.uk (Hillside)

www.twsitelines.info/search – Tyne and Wear HER (7580) (1586) and (13219)

www.ancestry.co.uk

www.findmypast.co.uk

www.ndfhs.org.uk

www.newmp.org.uk

Index of Houses

* Indicates the house is no longer standing.